21 STRANGE ANIMALS

THAT LIVE IN THE RAINFOREST

SELENA DALE

21 STRANGE ANIMALS THAT LIVE IN THE RAINFOREST

BOOK 2

Selena Dale

FREE GIFTS!

Just to say thank you for purchasing this book, I want to give you some free gifts.

Collect your free gifts here:

www.selenadale.com/get-your-free-gifts

Table of Contents

Introduction

Introduction

Rainforests are amazing and beautiful. They contain more than half of the world's plant and animal species!

Rainforests are tall and very dense jungles that are teeming with awesome creatures. There are a lot of really strange animals that live in the rainy and very wet conditions of these huge forests. Many of them look as though they are from another planet and tend to have interesting habits.

Every year new and unusual animal species are being discovered which tells us there are even more strange creatures out there that we don't even know about...yet.

So what kind of weird and wonderful animals can we expect to find in different parts of the word?

What do these creatures look like and what do they eat?

What kind of habitat do they live in and most importantly...are they dangerous?

Sometimes an animal can look as though it is dangerous when in actual fact it is as gentle as a furry little kitten. Then again, there are animals that look so cute and cuddly yet they could be vicious killers!

So, here we have 21 strange animals that live in the rainforest. Some are a little weird, some are funny looking and some are dangerous but all of them are fascinating to learn about.

Click on the images if you want to enlarge them.

1. KINKAJOU

As inhabitants of the forests of Central and South America, Kinkajous are omnivores and are often found in trees.

Kinkajous are close relatives of raccoons and are sometimes called "Honey Bears" because they are fond of raiding the nests of bees.

They are nocturnal beings, which means that they eat and roam around at night and are often asleep during daytime.

FUN FACT: A Kinkajou's tail is very useful. It helps them hang on trees and helps in improving their balance as it easily grips on branches.

2. POISON DART FROG

You have to beware of the Poison Dart Frog as it is one of the most toxic animals on the planet. In fact, its venom is capable of killing at 10 least 10 adults!

They are also able to make use of their colors as it helps them ward of strangers and enemies.

But, no matter how seemingly "evil" they are, they are actually good and caring parents to their offspring—they carry their offspring with them on their backs!

FUN FACT: The Poison Dart Frog is named as such because American-Indian tribes were fond of using them to poison their arrows.

3. BULLET ANT

Small but definitely terrible, the Bullet Ant is known to give the most painful sting in the whole world.

The Bullet Ant is often found in Nicaraguan Rainforests and is often fat, club-shaped and reddish-black. Some people even think that they are wasps because they look almost the same way.

FUN FACT: A rite of passage ritual conducted by the Satre-Mawe tribe in Brazil includes asking young men to be bitten by bullet ants for 20 times in a day! Yikes!

4. JESUS LIZARD

The Jesus Lizard is also known as the Great Basilisk Lizard. It comes from the family of iguanas and is an excellent swimmer.

Its tail can also act as a whip in times of danger and helps protect it against enemies. An adult Jesus Lizard can grow up to 2 feet long.

FUN FACT: The Jesus Lizard got its moniker from Jesus. It is able to run on water, the way Jesus was able to walk on water—like a miracle of nature!

5. PEANUT HEAD BUG

The Peanut Head Bug is named as such because its head resembles a peanut.

This works for them because predators think that they are not edible and so they choose to hunt for other prey. They also look like large bugs when their wings are spread out.

FUN FACT: While they may look terrifying, Peanut Head Bugs do not bite. All they can do is suck plant juices and that's why they rely on their weird appearance to keep them safe.

6. SATANIC LEAF TAILED GECKO

The Satanic Leaf Tailed Gecko often roams around the rainforests of Eastern Madagascar and really good at camouflaging themselves, making it hard for predators to find or notice them.

Its tail looks like a leaf and that's why it's so easy for it to blend with its surroundings. It is also often deemed as unique because of its physical appearance.

FUN FACT: While seemingly scary, the Satanic Gold Leaf Gecko is actually the smallest Gecko in the world!

7. PROBOSCIS MONKEY

The Proboscis Monkey is a very dominant type of monkey that is often found in the forests of Borneo.

They have webbed toes and the stomach of both males and females resembles a pot belly. They are full of fur that protect them from harsh weather conditions and also other animals.

FUN FACT: While you may think that its nose is ugly, it is actually what helps the Proboscis Monkey to find and attract a mate!

8. AYE-AYE

It is said that an Aye-Aye, (which is a type of lemur), is related to apes, chimpanzees and even humans.

They can be found in Madagascar and are mostly active at night. They eat insect larva, nectar, seeds, fruit and fungi.

They use their specially designed extra long middle finger to pick out food from inside tree trunks or hard shells.

FUN FACT: You won't find Aye-Ayes on the ground as they spend most of their lives clinging on to trees. They do not like going down and mingling with other animals.

9. GLASS FROG

At first you may think that the Glass Frog is just your average frog because it's in the color of lime green. But, take a good look at its stomach and you'll see that it is transparent, just like glass.

They often live near forest streams in Costa Rica and Central America and they are very active during daytime. They make use of that time to breed.

FUN FACT: You'll know that a frog is a glass frog if you see that its eyes are always facing forward and are very bright, especially during night-time.

10. POTOO

If you're traveling in Central and South America, you may already have come across a Potoo without knowing it. This is because a Potoo is one of the best animals in the world when it comes to camouflaging.

It could easily be mistaken for a small tree stump. These birds often lay their eggs on tree stumps to protect them from ground animals.

FUN FACT: While now common in South America, Potoos were first found in France and Germany 23 million years ago!

11. COLUGO

The Colugo is also known as the Sunda Flying Lemur and is often found in Borneo's jungles. They are great gliders and use the flaps between their legs to move from tree to tree.

Their teeth are quite destructive and they are nocturnal beings who are shy.

FUN FACT: As babies, Colugos spend around 6 months of their life clinging to their mother's bellies for protection.

12. AXOLOTL

A salamander that looks way different from other salamanders, the Axolotl is charming—due to its light pink (almost translucent) color, feathery gills and the fuzzes on its head.

Even when it has grown up, it still looks like a larva or a tadpole and are exclusively found in Xochimilco, Mexico.

They also tend to live in canals and lakes. They grow to up a foot long.

FUN FACT: Axolotls stay mainly underwater—unlike other salamanders who like to perch on rocks or on land, at times.

13. OKAPI

The Okapi is a Zebra Giraffe that is native to Congo. With their reddish-black body and white stripes, they look like zebras especially from a distance but are closer relatives of the Giraffe.

Like Giraffes, they are fond of eating buds and leaves of trees and don't like spending time with other animals.

FUN FACT: The Okapi has quite a long tongue. It uses its tongue to clean its ears (inside-out!) and even its eyelids!

14. RHINOCEROS HORNBILL

The Rhinoceros Hornbill is one of the largest of its kind and it can be found in Asian Rainforests.

It is popular for having red or orange irises and are often found inside tree trunks, especially if females are pregnant.

They are also quite protective of their hiding places, making sure that no other animals are able to go in.

FUN FACT: The Rhinoceros Hornbill is fond of eating small reptiles more than it likes fruits or insects.

15. DECOY-BUILDING SPIDER

A new species of spiders have recently been discovered in the Peruvian Amazon rainforests as part of the Genus Cyclosa.

The Decoy-Building Spider creates fake spiders and places them on their web in order to let predators think that these are real. The predators would come along and attack the decoy instead of the real spider.

FUN FACT: Interestingly enough, the decoy spiders do not just look like real spiders, they can also seem like they move! Weird!

16. CAPYBARA

Known as the largest rodent in the world, the Capybara is native to South America and is a close relative of guinea pigs.

They often roam around with a group of 10-100 Capybaras.

They are total herbivores who eat plants only and do not even like the smell of meat!

FUN FACT: Capybaras are awesome swimmers and divers. They can stay underwater for as long as 5 minutes!

17. THE PUSS CATERPILLAR

What makes the Puss Caterpillar different from other caterpillars is the fact that it is overly fuzzy and hairy.

The Puss Caterpillar is often found in the rainforests of Mexico and Central America. Be careful with this insect as its sting really hurts and can cause skin irritation and may even numb your limbs and bones!

FUN FACTS: It is usually gray or golden-brown and often looks like it hasn't brushed its hair. Now that's one animal that always has a bad hair day!

18. THE PINK DOLPHIN

Also known as the Pink Amazon River Dolphin, you cannot find dolphins such as this in the Ocean.

Aside from being Pink, sometimes they have flecks of brown or gray on their skin, too. They also should not be hunted as they are already close to extinction.

FUN FACTS: Pink Dolphins are the most intelligent of all dolphins! That's one more reason why they should be kept safe and taken care of.

19. 24 HOUR ANT

A close relative of the bullet ant, the 24 hour ant is infamous in Venezuela.

Their sting can truly hurt and may cause you to feel extreme pain and may make you feel numb for at least 24 hours, thus the name.

FUN FACT: While the Angel Falls is a popular tourist attraction in Venezuela, you have to be wary of 24-hour ants as they also frequent the place a lot.

20. HONDURAN WHITE BAT

The Honduran White Bat is probably the cutest and tiniest kind of bat that you will see. It has a white and fluffy coat and has almost no hair.

They are also called "leaf-nosed" bats at times because of the appearance of their nose and are often found in Nicaragua and the Honduras.

FUN FACT: The black membrane that covers their skull is quite useful: It is a natural form of sunscreen that protects them from the harsh rays of the sun!

21. MATA MATA

A large, freshwater turtle that is found in South Africa, the Mata-Mata is the only existing species in the Chelus Genus.

It is spiky and has large scales and often camouflages itself as a bark of a tree to ward off predators.

It uses its snout to breathe when it is in the water and is often found in stagnant pools or blackwater streams.

FUN FACT: While it has a large mouth, the Mata-Mata cannot chew and only swallows its food whole!

About Selena

Selena Dale was born in United Kingdom, London and has lived there most of her life. She has a passion for writing and loves to learn new things, especially if she can share what she has learned with her two children.

Due to her varied interests and love of writing she decided to create children's books. She can now pick and choose any topic to write about while sharing what she has written with her kids.

"Young children's brains are like sponges, ready to absorb all that wonderful knowledge. A child who loves to read is a child whose imagination will be flexed like a muscle. Now that is a pretty good foundation."

Selena Dale

Check Out My Other Books

Just go to Amazon and search for "Selena Dale Books"

OR

Got to www.selenadale.com

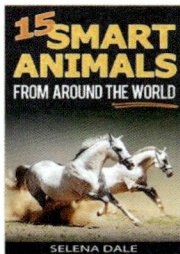

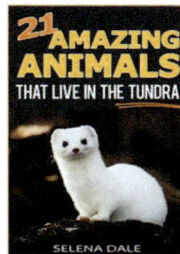

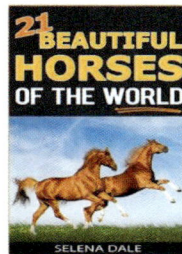

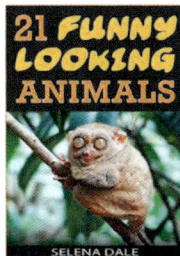

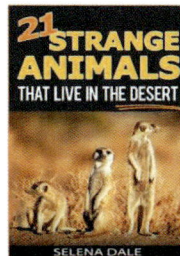

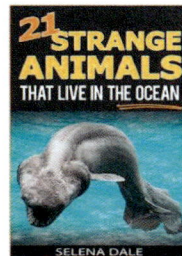

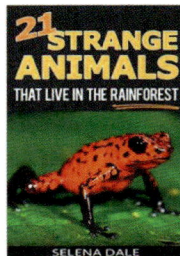

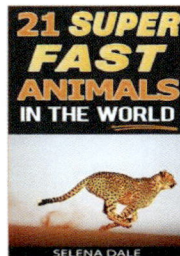

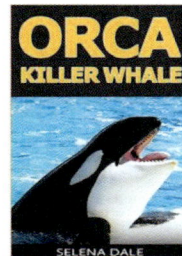

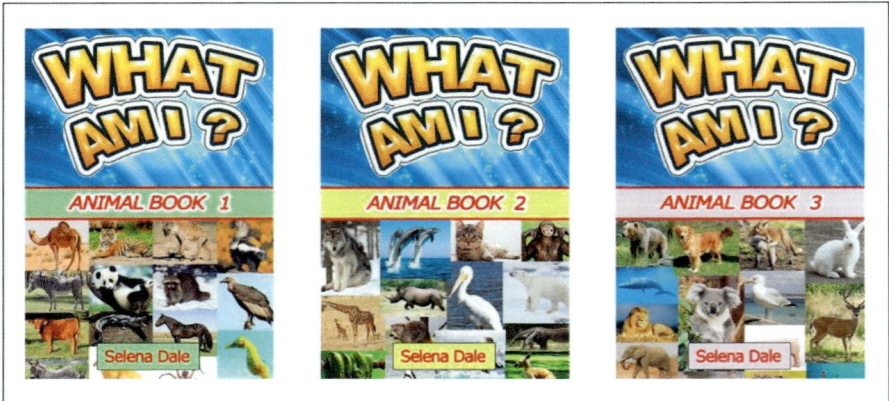

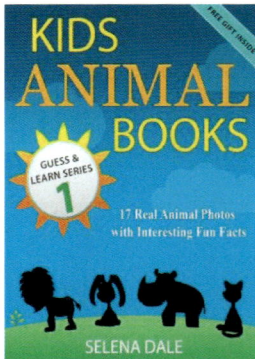

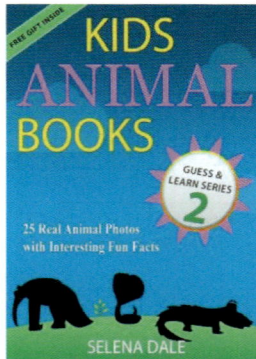

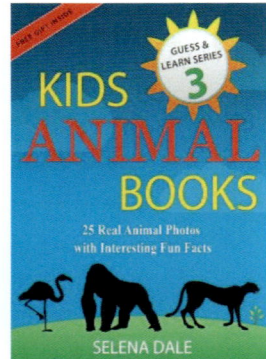

MANY MORE FUN CHILDREN'S BOOKS COMING SOON!

IMAGE SOURCE AUTHORS

16779676R00026

Printed in Poland
by Amazon Fulfillment
Poland Sp. z o.o., Wrocław